A PEOPLE CALLED EPISCOPALIANS

A Brief Introduction to Our Way of Life

REVISED EDITION

JOHN H. WESTERHOFF with SHARON ELY PEARSON

Morehouse Publishing
NEW YORK

Unless otherwise noted, the Scripture quotations contained herein are from the New Revised Standard Version Bible, copyright © 1989 by the Division of Christian Education of the National Council of Churches of Christ in the U.S.A. Used by permission. All rights reserved.

This book was originally published as *A People Called Episcopalians: A Brief Introduction to Our Peculiar Way of Life* © 2002, Morehouse Publishing.

Pages 39: Glossary adapted from *An Episcopal Dictionary of the Church: A User-Friendly Reference for Episcopalians*, Don S. Armentrout, Robert Boak Slocum, editors, copyright ©1999 Church Publishing and The Book of Common Prayer.

With thanks to the contributions of Tobias Stanislas Haller BSG

Morehouse Publishing, 4785 Linglestown Road, Suite 101, Harrisburg, PA 17112

Morehouse Publishing, 19 East 34th Street, New York, NY 10016

Morehouse Publishing is an imprint of Church Publishing Incorporated.
www.churchpublishing.org

Cover design by Laurie Klein Westhafer
Typeset by Linda Brooks

Library of Congress Cataloging-in-Publication Data
A catalog record of this book is available from the Library of Congress.

ISBN-13: 978-0-8192-3188-8 (pbk.)
ISBN-13: 978-0-8192-3189-5 (ebook)

Printed in Canada

CONTENTS

Introduction

Almighty Father, whose blessed Son before his passion prayed for his disciples that they might be one, as you and he are one: Grant that your Church, being bound together in love and obedience to you, may be united in one body by the one Spirit, that the world may believe in him whom you have sent, your Son Jesus Christ our Lord; who lives and reigns with you, in the unity of the Holy Spirit, one God, now and for ever. Amen.

COLLECT FOR THE UNITY OF THE CHURCH (BCP, P. 255)

Episcopalians pray this prayer for the unity of the Church so that we all may be one. The Episcopal Church is one of many Christian traditions, each of which maintains its particular and distinct identity as they each strive to best live into their baptism and grow in their relationship to God. Each denomination and branch of the Christian family tree recognizes the unique contribution the other can make to the whole.

Today Episcopalians come from an increasing diverse collection of Christians from varied backgrounds (70 percent come to us from other traditions) who gather around shared convictions about prayer, liturgy, church government, and—most importantly—the life and ministry of Jesus Christ. We're a place that welcomes random questions and eccentric personalities. We're a peculiar people whose spiritual arc bends more towards boundless hope and a reasonable faith than hardened surety and entrenched absolutism.

For four hundred years, Episcopalians have found comfort, nurture, fellowship, and encouragement in our faith communities. And we believe the Almighty is not finished with us yet. We believe—now more than ever—that we provide a uniquely fulfilling and vital role in the panoply of modern Christian experiences. If we Episcopalians are to participate fully in the vision of Church union, we will need to become more conscious of what it means to be Episcopal Christians.

What follows is intended to address the foundational issue of who is the Episcopal Church and what are the convictions that hold us together as Episcopalians, offering a stimulus for conversation among us. These brief essays, while not intending to be authoritative, can become a resource for study and reflection between and among those who are Episcopalians and those who are inquiring about becoming part of this family of faith that we call the Episcopal Church.

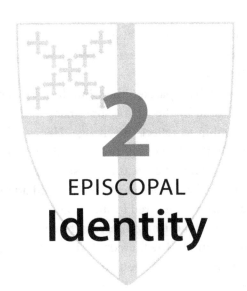

EPISCOPAL
Identity

Almighty God, you have built your Church upon the foundation of the apostles and prophets, Jesus Christ himself being the chief cornerstone: Grant us so to be joined together in unity of spirit by their teaching, that we may be made a holy temple acceptable to you; through Jesus Christ our Lord, who lives and reigns with you and the Holy Spirit, one God, for ever and ever. Amen.

COLLECT FOR PROPER 8 (BCP, P. 230)

The Episcopal tradition, like every other Christian tradition, is founded on the affirmation that Jesus Christ is Lord. That affirmation is essential to the foundation of the unity of the Church. As Episcopalians, we believe that Christ's **transcendent** presence in the Holy Spirit has continually formed, reformed, informed, and transformed who we are as one branch of the tree, which is the Christian church.

The Episcopal Church is a descendant of the Church of England, which was itself founded in 597 as a mission outpost of the Roman Catholic Church, through St. Augustine of Canterbury at the direction of Pope St. Gregory the Great. A variety of factors led to the parting of the ways between England and Rome some five hundred years ago, and it's one that we're still working to heal. Many of the rituals, traditions, and ways of believing in Christ have been passed down to us through the Roman Catholic strand of our heritage.

When King Henry VIII separated the Church of England from the authority of the Roman Catholic Church by the Act of Supremacy in 1534, it became necessary to revise the Church's worship to reflect the change. Henry told Archbishop Thomas Cranmer that he wanted all liturgical books revised and written "in our native English tongue." "The Book of Common Prayer" was established in 1548 as the official worship book for the Church. This, and all subsequent editions and adaptations, including the one used by Episcopalians is often referred to simply as "the BCP."

As such, our Episcopal **tradition** represents the continuous tradition of the one, holy catholic, and apostolic church. The Episcopal Church has consistently been labeled a "middle road"—a *"via media"*—between Roman Catholicism and Protestantism. Originally and officially it is known as the Protestant (meaning not Roman Catholic or Orthodox) Episcopal (paradoxically meaning not Protestant) Church.

Our primary identity is as a community of practice. That is, we are bound together by our **liturgy** rather than doctrinal emphasis, or social organization. Orthodoxy for us is right worship and not right belief. Our life of prayer shapes our beliefs and behaviors.

In other branches of Christianity, the decisions of councils, the writings of particular theologians, catechisms, confessional doctrinal statements, the decisions of bishops, particular interpretations of Scripture, and polity have significance unknown to Episcopalians. To know what Episcopalians believe about issues of faith and life, all one needs to do is turn to the Book of Common Prayer and engage in the process of discovering the wealth of tradition and liturgy. We shape our understanding of faith and life through participation in our liturgies, and we reform our understandings and ways of life by reforming our liturgies. We are constantly seeking to hear the Spirit moving among us as changes in the historical development of our understandings of Christian belief and practice are seen through additional liturgical resources and revisions to the Book of Common Prayer.

Within the Episcopal Church, our styles of worship in different congregations may be quite diverse, but our substance and content are consistent. You may encounter the terms High Church and Low Church, although they are somewhat less common than when they were in style in the nineteenth and twentieth centuries. These reflect to some extent how the clergy are vested and whether incense is used (or not). Other terms used are "Anglo-Catholic" and "Evangelical." These concern more than just worship style, although the differing emphasis of each tradition is reflected in worship. While many churches fall somewhere in between all of these descriptors, in most cases it is a question of style and emphasis, rather than content. The Gospel is ultimately the Gospel.

No matter its style in the Episcopal Church, liturgy is the "work of the people." Episcopal liturgy is communal worship connected to our daily life and work as ministry. We bring the reverence and rootedness of an ancient liturgical tradition alongside a clear devotion to the Bible. Although we have ordained ministers (including the bishops that give us our name—Episcopal), we also value the shared ministry of all believers.

People join the Episcopal Church for many reasons. For some, it has been the church of their family for generations. For others it may be because of our views on Holy Communion, women's ordination, and human rights. Some love the music; others love the liturgy. There is an atmosphere of open curiosity, allowing people to ask and answer questions, striving to let the Holy Spirit work among us.

3

EPISCOPAL

Authority

Lord of all power and might, the author and giver of all good things: Graft in our hearts the love of your Name; increase in us true religion; nourish us with all goodness; and bring forth in us the fruit of good works; through Jesus Christ our Lord, who lives and reigns with you and the Holy Spirit, one God, for ever and ever. Amen.

COLLECT FOR PROPER 17 (BCP, P. 233)

The word "authority" in the Episcopal sense refers to the author or source for our life of faith. Clearly God as revealed in Jesus Christ through the Holy Spirit is our ultimate, supreme, and sole authority. We are called upon to know the mind of the triune God fully so that we might do the will of God perfectly.

However, the question is, how do we come to know the mind of this triune God? The answer is to be found in our understanding of authority and how it functions. Without this common authority and agreement upon how it is used, there is no way to maintain a common life, especially when persons and groups arrive at different conclusions.

Our understanding of authority is deeply rooted in our history. During the time of the English Reformation in the sixteenth century, the Church of England became a political identity, which is the one, holy, catholic, and apostolic church in England. At the time there were two divergent understandings of authority within the Christian church. Roman Catholic Christians maintained a dual authority for discerning the mind of God, namely Scripture and tradition, with the emphasis being placed on tradition (the authoritative teachings of the church, which resulted from the bishops' interpretations of the Holy Scriptures). Protestant Christians, on the other hand, contended that the Scriptures alone were the authority of the church and that the meaning of the Scriptures was to be determined without recourse to any established tradition. Indeed, tradition was to play no role in determining the mind and will of God. Only what was contained in the Scriptures was to have any authority.

Rather than take sides, the Church of England (whose members are called **Anglicans**) asserted that the Scriptures contain all that is needed to be known for salvation. (The "Articles of Religion" were written in 1571.) Therefore, one need not believe anything that is *not* in the Scriptures; one might, however, believe anything that is not *incompatible* with the Scriptures. For example, Anglicans may believe (as Roman Catholics do) in the assumption of Mary, a doctrine not denied in the Scriptures; yet Anglicans do not *have* to believe in this doctrine (as Protestants do not), for it is not a doctrine contained in the Scriptures. Another way of stating this middle-way position is to say that revelation as contained in the Scriptures about God and God's will is essential to our salvation, but revelation in the Scriptures is not the source of all our knowledge about God and God's will.

Churches that trace their origin to the Church of England have often revised and produce prayer books of their own to reflect their own national circumstances and languages. The Episcopal Church separated from the Church of England at the time of the American Revolution and published its first Book of Common Prayer, based on both the English and Scottish prayer books. Further revisions to the American book were made in 1892, 1928, and most extensively in 1979.

Episcopalians will say our theology is like a three-legged stool, needing each leg in order to be balanced. This comes from Richard Hooker, an Anglican theologian who, in *The Laws of Ecclesiastical Polity* (Book Two, 1534), advocated for a diffuse authority composed of three interrelated, dependent, authoritative sources: Scripture, tradition, and reason. This understanding has become the hallmark of our unique Episcopal (and Anglican) understanding of authority.

Hooker argued that while the Scriptures are to be our primary source of authority, they are not to be isolated from reason and tradition. Why? Because God communicated his revelation as contained in the Scriptures in a manner sensitive to the specific needs of a specific group in a specific time in history and, therefore, intended that they be interpreted to make sense to a different people in a different time. God's revelation was, therefore, to be both inside and outside of the Scriptures, guarded and guided by the Holy Spirit. The Scriptures are intended, Hooker asserted, to be a living word and not a collection of dead letters. That is, the Scriptures (and tradition) are not self-explanatory but require the use of reason to determine their meaning. Reason, of course, is not autonomous or individualistic. Nor are there three different authorities. Rather, there is a single authority composed of three intersecting sources: the Scriptures being the normative authoritative source; reason and tradition being necessary interpretive authoritative sources.

The implications of this understanding are profound. While maintaining that the Scriptures provide us with a unifying plumb line, Episcopalians are willing to live with diverse and changing interpretations, rather than infallible certainty and binding prescriptions for all times.

The Holy Scriptures

As *The Outline of the Faith* (also know as the *Catechism*) in the Book of Common Prayer (p. 845-862) explains it, the Holy Scriptures are called the Word of God "because God still speaks to us through the Bible." God inspired people to write and continues to speak to us through what they wrote. Thus the biases, preferences, and prejudices of these authors, as well as their cultural understandings, are to some degree present in the Bible we have today. This does not make the Bible any less "true" but it does help us better to understand the human side of the work by which it came to be. We understand their meaning through the aid of the Holy Spirit, who guides the Church in their true interpretation.

Revelation is God's self-disclosure to persons and communities. The Scriptures are a record of that revelation. That is, they contain God's revelation, but they are not to be confused with the revelation itself.

As the Scriptures were written and edited over a long period of time, their writers and editors were in conversation with earlier, spoken traditions and written documents, quoting them, allegorizing them, correcting them, harmonizing them, interpreting and reinterpreting them, as well as adding new material. There is no doubt that these holy men and women, moved by God, participated in bringing these great writings to us. So Episcopalians tend to see the Bible's origins less as a divine product with divine authorship and more as a response to the presence and action of God.

The Scriptures, as the Church finally established them as **canon**—its measuring rod or standard for the Christian life of faith—were understood as living, fluid records of the community's experience of God over time and therefore carried more meanings than their immediate and plain literal sense. These writings are literary, historical documents in need of critical examination and interpretation. As might be expected, controversies over interpretation developed even as they were being written (and continue to this day). For the first 1,500 years of the church's history, the primary authority became the tradition, that is, the authorized interpretations of the Church, rather than the literal words of specific texts. The real issue for the church now is not whether the Scriptures have authority (of course, they do) but how they are read and heard within the Church.

Episcopalians are exposed to considerable portions of Scripture during worship. The Lectionary, a selection of Scripture readings appointed for Sunday worship (the Daily Office also has a lectionary for corporate or private worship) spreads out the readings over a three-year cycle. Each Sunday we hear a portion of Scripture from the Old Testament, Psalter (Psalms), New Testament, and Gospels.

As a Church that adheres to a history of scriptural tradition, Episcopalians have never held to a doctrine of biblical supremacy (no other source of knowledge has value), literal interpretation (everything is literally true), or verbal inerrancy (God wrote each and every word). Rather, we have always supported all forms of biblical scholarship and accepted diverse opinions. While holding the Scriptures in high regard, we do not describe them as having ultimate authority in all matters. For example, we allow science to inform us as to how the world was created. The creation stories answer why and by whom. Nor do we assert that everything found within them is binding on us. For example, we do not follow Old Testament dietary laws. Further, Episcopalians do not believe that the Scriptures provide specific, final judgments on every moral and theological issue or questions. One example is that the writers were unaware of the possibility of genetics and they misunderstood how babies were conceived.

Importantly, we believe that the Scriptures are to be taken as a whole. No one part of Scripture (such as a verse) is to be taken in isolation from the whole. Each is to be heard in relationship to other themes and passages. We are not literalists or legalists, so we avoid proof-texting, which is using single passages for theological or ethical conclusions.

The penchant we have for comprehension (rather than compromise) comes to us as spiritual progeny of the Church of England. We have inherited this English proclivity toward finding middle ground between two extremes. As Episcopalians discern our way forward on issues of the day, we consider these three sources of Anglican authority on the subject at hand: Scripture, tradition (including theology, liturgy, canon law, and history), and reason (including our human experience). This *via media*, middle way, helps us focus on the work of proclaiming the Gospel of Jesus Christ, being open and willing to listen with honest dialogue as we try to understand how best to live up to God's revelation in today's world.

Tradition

When Episcopalians talk about tradition as part of our "three-legged stool," we are referring to the many ways that the saints before us have dealt with issues of faith and doctrine. As we discern the mind and will of God in our reading of the Scriptures, we recognize that they were formed and interpreted throughout history. As Paul wrote, "For I handed on to you of first importance what I in turn had received . . ." (1 Corinthians 15:3a). It was an oral tradition, and the liturgies and practices of the early church were used in the formation of the New Testament. Further, insofar as these Scriptures did not speak plainly or clearly on all issues, and by their nature required interpretation, the wisdom of the community throughout history has always been an important guide to our life of faith in the present.

Tradition, of course, is much more than the history of interpretation of the Scriptures. Tradition, for Episcopalians, is also expressed in our liturgies with their prayers, appointed collects, lessons, and hymns. Tradition's role is to guard and give witness to the Scriptures, especially through worship as we continue to discern the mind and will of God. Just as the Scriptures inform tradition, tradition informs Scripture.

We give special attention to the first five centuries of the Christian church. These are the formative years of the church in which the canon of the Scriptures was established, seven ecumenical councils were held, the creeds were established, and the work of classical theologians—the "church fathers"—gave us their various imaginative means for interpreting the Scriptures.

Tradition also includes more modern things, such as bishops' pastoral letters and the actions of **General Conventions** (our governing body), the **Constitution and Canons** of the Episcopal Church, and historic documents such as the "Articles of Religion" (see p. 863-878 of the Book of Common Prayer for many such documents) and catechisms, along with various editions of our authorized hymnals. It is a tradition inclusive of elements from Orthodox, Roman Catholic, and Protestant traditions, but has many of its own distinctive elements.

Just as the church is not infallible, neither is tradition; it, too, must be interpreted continually and open to reform. It is important to acknowledge that we Episcopalians are a people who at the moment of our baptism are incorporated into a living, changing tradition, established by a community of faith that continually strives to know and do the will of God through the use of its three authoritative sources: Scripture, tradition, and reason. Such efforts cannot help but result in disagreement and creative tension within the church. Therefore, the church must be held together finally by the authority of love, or as Paul would advise us, "I therefore, the prisoner in the Lord, beg you to lead a life worthy of the calling to which you have been called, with all humility and gentleness, with patience, bearing with one another in love, making every effort to maintain the unity of the Spirit in the bond of peace." (Ephesians 4:1-3)

Reason

A necessary tool in understanding both Scripture and our tradition is reason. **Reason** involves both common sense and the wisdom to draw on the very broadest scope of human understanding, along with the deep well of personal experience. It plays a significant role in that it provides the means by which we express and communicate God's revelation. Reason is the divinely implanted faculty for receiving and understanding the divine revelation. It is the *rational mind* that is traditionally designated as the residence of the Divine Image in human beings. For Episcopalians, human reason was never totally corrupted by the fall (Genesis 3), but only weakened, and God's grace has been ever present to our rational minds, making it possible for God's Spirit to lead us into truth. While our use of reason can distort and deny the mind and heart of God, it can also discern and comprehend it.

However, reason is not limited solely to an intellectual way of thinking and knowing that turns all of reality into an object for human investigation and manipulation. Reason is more than logical analysis. It includes the intuitive way of thinking and knowing and is therefore prayerful, contemplative reflection on contemporary human experience and knowledge in the light of the Scriptures and tradition. Understood this way, reason is the means by which the Holy Spirit works within the church to enable it to discern the mind and will of God. Reason requires the revelation contained in the Scriptures and to which tradition attests, but revelation requires the use of reason if it is to inform and influence the life of faith.

Rationalism—an excessive concern for the sole use of the intellect—deviates from an Episcopal ethos, as does anti-intellectualism and the denial of the use of the intellect regarding religious subjects and an excessive concern for right feelings and emotions. Reason remains our God-given means for understanding the Scriptures and tradition and discerning the working of God's Spirit in present experience. Emphasizing both the intellectual and intuitive ways of thinking and knowing, reason assumes and employs contemporary human experience or consciousness as a doorway into the mind and heart of God in the past and present.

Reason is far from perfect, and it cannot on its own bring us to faith. There are some truths that cannot be proved, but only believed, including some of the truths revealed by Scripture which reason can understand, but not demonstrate.

Authority and Community

In its being, the Episcopal Church can be seen as living out our understanding of authority in our diversity of theological, liturgical, ethical, and pastoral viewpoints. At least four communities of "emphasis" can be recognized in how the Episcopal Church affirms the appropriate roles of the Scriptures, tradition, and reason. Those from an Evangelical perspective remind us of the centrality of the Holy Scriptures and the truths of the Protestant reformers for our common life. Anglo-Catholics remind us of the place of tradition and the truths of the Roman Catholic and Orthodox Christians for our church. Liberals—composed of many of our systematic theologians, ethicists, and social activists—surface to remind us of the importance of the human experience, the use of reason, and the truth that comes from outside the church. Those who consider themselves "Broad Church" remind us that if any of the others dominate or exclude another we will fall into heresy—either from Biblicism, traditionalism, or rationalism. The stool will topple over.

While each voice has an essential contribution to make, none can dominate or diminish the important place of the others. Each needs to consider seriously the insights of the others. Each needs to listen carefully to and reflect prayerfully on the convictions of the others. Each needs to believe that another may have discerned the mind and will of God more fully than itself. Each needs to be open to the working of the Holy Spirit and be willing to change long-held convictions if the community as a whole comes to a new discernment. And all must be committed to the unity of the church.

While **lay persons**, bishops, priests, deacons, dioceses, or congregations may have a particular leaning, we are all obliged to live peacefully and constructively with our differences until we can achieve consensus or live with our differences, praying together and for each other until God helps us to reconcile them.

As Paul reminds us, we are one body with many members. Such is the body of Christ.

> *Now you are the body of Christ and individually members of it. And God has appointed in the church first apostles, second prophets, third teachers; then deeds of power, then gifts of healing, forms of assistance, forms of leadership, various kinds of tongues. Are all apostles? Are all prophets? Are all teachers? Do all work miracles? Do all possess gifts of healing? Do all speak in tongues? Do all interpret? But strive for the greater gifts. And I will show you a still more excellent way.* (1 Corinthians 12:12-31)

EPISCOPAL
Spirituality

Heavenly Father, in you we live and move and have our being: We humbly pray you so to guide and govern us by your Holy Spirit, that in all the cares and occupations of our life we may not forget you, but may remember that we are ever walking in your sight; through Jesus Christ our Lord. Amen.

A COLLECT FOR GUIDANCE (BCP, P. 100)

Despite our authority resting in Scripture, tradition, and reason, what holds the body of the Episcopal Church together is our common prayer. Our spiritual life is ordinary everyday life lived in an ever deepening and loving relationship with God and therefore with our true self, all others, and creation. Prayer is the many and varied means by which that relationship is enhanced and enlivened. Our intimate communication with God can occur before a meal, at bedtime, during a worship service, or any time the need or opportunity arises. Spoken aloud or silently, it is taking time to listen to what God is saying to us. Episcopal spirituality—our approach to growth in this relationship with God—has numerous characteristics, which together compose our distinctive life of prayer.

Liturgical and Biblical

Episcopal spirituality is rooted in daily prayer: Morning Prayer, Noonday Prayer, Evening Prayer, and Compline—all found in the **Book of Common Prayer**. Communal prayer in the Episcopal Church tends to be more formal and ritualistic than prayer in many other traditions. These services of prayer are ordered by the Gospel narrative as manifested in the church year with its season and emphases of readings and prayers.

We pray to build and shape our relationship with God. We are a tradition that believes in a daily discipline of formal ritual prayer, composed of a variety of forms: adoration, praise, thanksgiving, penitence, oblation, intercession, and petition with a focus upon the prayerful engagement with the Scriptures. Episcopalians might easily rule out any spiritual practices that neglected the Scriptures.

Communal

Communal prayer always comes before personal prayer, as the first informs the second. While we maintain the importance of personal prayer, we hold a continuing concern that prayer not become individualistic or privatized. Prayers of intercession are central to our common life and are part of every worship experience, whether it is the Holy Eucharist, Morning Prayer, or any other rite in the Book of Common Prayer. We follow a communal calendar of feasts and fasts that assigns persons and events to be remembered so as to help focus our personal spiritual lives. Through prayer with our tradition, our personal spiritual lives are enriched.

Whenever Episcopalians gather for a meeting, before making a decision, or any communal gathering, the community gathers in the context of communal prayer and meditation so that the Holy Spirit might inform and influence our time together. We are also prone to wait for consensus rather than make win/lose decisions, prayerfully listening to and pondering the discernment of others, especially the least among us. Further, any discernment, personal or corporate, needs confirmation by others.

Sacramental

Episcopalians understand the **sacraments** as outward and visible signs of inward and spiritual grace. Grace is God's favor towards us, unearned and undeserved, given by God for our benefit. For Episcopalians there are two great sacraments, given to us by Christ: Holy **Baptism** and the Holy **Eucharist**. Other sacramental rites, which evolved in the Church under the guidance of the Holy Spirit, include confirmation (or baptismal reaffirmation), ordination, holy matrimony, **reconciliation of a penitent**, and unction (anointing of the sick and dying). These traditions are symbolic in usage and action. We depend on the sacraments and sacramental actions to make Christ present to us and to make us aware of God's presence and action in our lives and those of others.

Through baptism, God adopts us as children and makes us members of Christ's Body, the Church. The outward and visible sign in Holy Baptism is water in which the person is baptized in the name of the Father, and of the Son, and of the Holy Spirit. The Book of Common Prayer affirms the practice of infant baptism, reminding us that the community's faith comes before ours, that God's grace is given to us before we respond, that participation in the sacraments grants us the gift of faith. We are always living into the reality of our baptism, becoming who we already are. Parents and godparents (sponsors) make promises on behalf of infants as the whole witnessing community renews their own promises as found in the Baptismal Covenant. Baptism is full membership into Christ's Church. In the Episcopal Church, all baptized persons, regardless of age, are welcome to receive Holy Communion.

Participation in the sacrament of the Holy Eucharist on a weekly basis is also emphasized in the Episcopal Church. Each week we come together to experience life in God's reign, where all people are restored to unity with God and each other in Christ, and where God's will is known and done. We are asked to examine our lives, repent of our sins, and be in love and charity with all people when we come to the Lord's Table. Through our participation in this sacramental action of sharing bread and wine, we are reconstituted as Christ's body, infused with Christ's life, and empowered to be Christ's presence in the world. We leave each service of Holy Communion renewed so that we return to our daily lives and work as a sign and witness to God's reign.

The Episcopal Church uses a variety of names for this liturgy: Holy Eucharist, the Lord's Supper, Holy Communion, the Divine Liturgy, the Mass, and the Great Offering. No matter what we call our worship, our sacramental spirituality informs our conviction that just as Christ was the sacrament of God, the Church is called to be the sacrament of Christ in the world. Our spirituality is contemplative and active, inward and outward.

Pastoral

As Episcopalians, we recognize particular moments in the lives of individual Christians through rites under the auspices of the Pastoral Offices. Unlike the Eucharist, Baptism, and the Daily Offices (Morning Prayer, etc.) that are integrated into the celebration of the liturgical year, the Episcopal Church also offers services that are geared to the pattern of individual lives. These include the rite of Confirmation, Reception and Reaffirmation of baptismal vows, the celebration and blessing of a marriage, thanksgiving for the birth or adoption of a child, reconciliation of a penitent, ministration to the sick as well as at the time of death, and burial of the dead. These appear in the Book of Common Prayer in roughly the order that individuals experience them.

These rites, the intercessions we regularly pray at worship, and our baptismal promises support a spirituality that maintains that our relationship with God is measured by our relationship with our true self, all people, and the natural world. Prayer as devotion to God and prayer as service to the neighbor in need go hand in hand.

Incarnational

Our emphasis on God's entry (Jesus Christ) into human life and history has resulted in an earthly spirituality. Jesus was fully human and fully divine, the Son of God "in the flesh." Ours is an **incarnational** faith. We believe that the extraordinary is to be found in the ordinary. We affirm life in this world and believe that the body, pleasure, and material reality are fundamentally good. This means that we are free to make choices: to love, to create, to reason, and to live in harmony with creation and with God. We believe that that natural world is God's good gift to us.

Part of God's creation, we are made in the image of God. What matters is what we do with and how we care for these gifts. We are to honor them, care for them, and share them with all people. Care for our physical health is an aspect of our spiritual life; so is fun, play, and pleasure.

Mystical

Mysticism is a particularly focused part of spirituality. In our human quest for the experience of union with God, Episcopalians are more inclined to a mystical path. This emphasizes a long, slow journey into union with God through spiritual discipline and prayer, a series of conversion experiences along life's journey, new convictions, and new commitments. Mysticism, and spirituality in general, seem to rise during times of intense change and stress.

While it cannot be said that Episcopalians never experience immediate encounters with God and the assurance of divine election through a single, dramatic emotional conversion experience (pietism), we tend to be open to the creative power of God working in and through us throughout our lives. Our mystical union with God may be found to be in simple contemplation of Holy Scripture.

EPISCOPAL
Temperament

O God, you made us in your own image and redeemed us through Jesus your Son: Look with compassion on the whole human family; take away the arrogance and hatred which infect our hearts; break down the walls that separate us; unite us in bonds of love; and work through our struggle and confusion to accomplish your purposes on earth; that, in your good time, all nations and races may serve you in harmony around your heavenly throne; through Jesus Christ our Lord. Amen.

FOR THE HUMAN FAMILY (BCP, P. 815)

Temperament refers to a tradition's characteristic ways of thinking and behaving. For Episcopalians, this is comprehensive, ambiguous, open-minded, intuitive, aesthetic, moderate, naturalistic, historical, and political.

Comprehensive

Episcopalians affirm a principle of *via media* (literally, nothing too much, or the middle way). This includes the conviction that truth is known and guarded by maintaining the tension between counter-opposite statements concerning truth. This principle is exemplified in the conviction that Jesus was fully human and at the same time fully divine, in the same commitment to being both fully Catholic and Protestant, and in the stated necessity of holding in tension personal freedom and communal responsibility. While applying this principle of comprehensiveness is extremely difficult to do in practice, the struggle to do so is an important part of the Episcopal tradition.

We affirm both the sacred and the secular; both the material and the nonmaterial nature of reality; the speculative illumination of the mind and the affective illumination of the heart; the possibility of a direct, unmediated experience of God, as well as the indirect mediated experience of God; and both the transcendent mystery of God and the immanent intimacy of God. We embrace the contradictory convictions that faith is a gift that results from participation in the sacraments and that faith is a necessary precondition for participation in the sacraments.

This principle provides a means to resolve what may appear to be severe disagreements in our beliefs and practices. For example, Episcopalians believe that we live into our baptism by the process of becoming who we already are. This may seem a conflicting statement, but we believe that every transformational benefit is given to us fully at our baptism and that we must engage throughout our lifetime in efforts to achieve the benefits of baptism, that is, union with Christ in his death and resurrection.

Ambiguous

This is a theological category that makes possible living with what may appear to be irreconcilable differences. When we are faced with new experiences or complex issues, we will remain open to various interpretations and demonstrate a willingness to live with uncertainty of meaning until a resolution can be found.

Episcopalians affirm an openness to all experience and believe in the developed capacity to be sensitive to and accept what our senses tell us even when it does not fit into a neat, comprehensible established category—whether it is ambiguous, incomprehensible, obscure, or strange. We are able to tolerate theological and ethical messiness; we do not need to have everything settled or resolved immediately. With a developed sensitivity we tend to be more inductive and pragmatic than deductive and systematic. We are willing to live with trial and error as a means toward establishing truth. Episcopalians believe that conflict, when handled in reconciling ways, is healthy and not to be avoided. Indeed, conflict is a necessary aspect of how Episcopalians theologically discern tasks, whether they involve ethical, social, liturgical, or political decisions.

This ability to live with ambiguity helps us to deal with situations in which two or more biblical texts, theological principles, or ethical norms appear logically incompatible. When this does occur, we are able to wait patiently—neither fleeing the situation nor fighting it—to pray with a discerning heart, and to listen with an open mind until the conflict can be reconciled through the aid of the Holy Spirit.

Open Minded

Episcopalians encourage a searching, questioning, reasonable mind always open to new insights and change. We listen carefully to everyone, search for wisdom everywhere, take seriously the secular world and its work, and recognize that contemporary knowledge is not necessarily in conflict with faith and indeed may offer wisdom. However, these character traits can result in the acceptance of all truth claims uncritically. It can also be used to avoid all decisions to what is good and true. We need to be careful to include all thoughts and not be selective, thereby opening the door to serious distortions.

Intuitive

While affirming the intellectual way of thinking and knowing, Episcopalians have also affirmed the intuitive way of thinking and knowing. We are at home with art as much as philosophy and the world of symbol, myth, and ritual. We are comfortable with liturgy that makes use of the arts such as drama, dance, music, poetry, and the visual arts. We are at ease with the "feminine" as well as "masculine" dimensions of life. Mystical, metaphorical, paradoxical, symbolic, and pre-rational are dimensions we explore in dealing with the human experience. Recognizing that human nature and society are more deeply motivated by images and tabulations than ideas and concepts, we are apt to emphasize imagination while keeping in tension the objective and rational with the subjective and non-rational.

Aesthetic

Truth, goodness, and beauty are related to each other in that the presence of one is judged by the presence of the other two. Beauty can be defined as a revelation of the presence (priestly) or the absence (prophetic) of goodness and truth. While some traditions emphasize truth or goodness, Episcopalians have made beauty the doorway to truth and goodness. We have a strong respect for and belief in the beauty of holiness and righteousness.

Our churches are designed with beauty and purpose in mind. In medieval times, craftsmen believed they were building sacred spaces to give glory to God, as well as to instruct the people in the history and mystery of faith. They were interested in creating an atmosphere of grandeur where people could sense God's presence. Stained glass windows found in many Episcopal churches, as well as many other church furnishings, remind us that the presence of beautiful objects can open our eyes to the wonders of God. Other visual aids include mural paintings, icons, statuary and relief carvings, and fabric art such as weavings and banners. Artists have always been at home in our congregations and play a significant role in our worship and common life.

Moderate

Episcopalians believe that they are called to live a godly (manifesting the divine image in ourselves), righteous (living in a right relationship to God and neighbor), and sober life. We are a people of moderation and restraint who strive to model a temperate, balanced, reasonable approach to life. It is a life in which prayer, work, study, and play have a rhythm and part.

Naturalistic

Having a reverence for and taking delight in the earthy rhythms of life, the seasons and their changes, the natural world and all of creation are another of the characteristics of an Episcopalian. We have affirmed historically natural theology and natural law—means by which God has made possible to all reasonable human beings some knowledge of God's will and ways—but we have always taken seriously the contributions of the natural sciences to human life. Through the years our poets have filled us with an awareness of nature and ecology. Caring for all of God's creation is something Episcopalians have long been interested in doing. At our best we have been committed to the protection of the environment and preserving the sanctity of creation. When the heavens and the earth were created, God called it good—and we believe it still is. This is why we seek to not only care for it, as God has, but to bless it, as God continues to do.

Historical

Episcopalians have a great sense of history and a desire to honor tradition. We respect what we can learn from a careful reflection on the past, as well as strive to maintain our roots in Anglican history and culture, going back further than our formation as the Episcopal Church following the American Revolution. This historic consciousness is manifested in our concern for an **historic episcopacy** in which our bishops are linked to the church and its past through apostolic succession.

Political

Lastly, our English history has made us a political church. We value the civic virtues and affirm free, peaceful, public debate as a basis for political unity. We believe that such civic debate should be encouraged and that the church is an appropriate place to engage in it. Just as we reflect on the writings of the prophets and the teachings of Jesus in Scripture, we believe that the church has an obligation to attempt to influence social, political, and economic life as a matter of justice and equality for all of God's people. We have always shown a concern for government, its policies and actions; an assumed responsibility for participation in public life; and accepted leadership role in politics.

One of the promises we make in our **Baptismal Covenant** is to "strive for justice and peace . . . and respect the dignity of every human being." (Book of Common Prayer, p. 304). You will find Episcopalians advocating on many justice issues, including war, the death penalty, and human rights. Most importantly, Episcopalians emphasize that our ministry—the context in which we serve God and represent Christ and his church—is our daily life and work.

6

EPISCOPAL
Polity

Almighty and everlasting God by whose Spirit the whole body of your faithful people is governed and sanctified: Receive our supplications and prayers, which we offer before you for all members of your holy Church, that in their vocation and ministry they may truly and devoutly serve you; through our Lord and Savior Jesus Christ, who lives and reigns with you, in the unity of the Holy Spirit, one God, now and forever. Amen.

FOR ALL CHRISTIANS IN THEIR VOCATION (BCP, P. 256)

A tradition's polity is its political structure and organization. If you were to look up the words "episcopal polity" in a dictionary, you will find something like this: "a hierarchical form of church governance where the chief local authorities are bishops whose presidency is both sacramental and political." That definition, however, is wrong for the Episcopal Church.

The Methodist Church is more nearly an episcopal church in the dictionary sense since its bishops have authority to assign clergy to a particular church. The Roman Catholic Church also is an episcopal church in some ways; its bishops have greater authority within their dioceses than do those of the Episcopal Church. Roman

Catholic bishops are also subject to the bishop of Rome (the Pope), so the government of the Roman Catholic Church is really "papal" rather than "episcopal."

Other polities within Christian bodies might be categorized as congregational and presbyterial. Congregational polity rests on the principle of governance by each and every member of a local, autonomous, independent congregation. Presbyterial polity rests on the principle of governance by elected representational bodies of clergy and laity ordered in a hierarchy.

The Episcopal Church rests on a principle of governance that combines elements of presbyterial and episcopal, but denies congregationalism. The Episcopal Church is not a church governed by bishops, but is governed by a combination of bishops, priests, deacons, and lay people elected by the membership of a church to take that responsibility. Our deep roots in a representative form of government can be attributed to the birth of the Episcopal Church coinciding with the birth of the United States. The constitutions of the nation and the Episcopal Church were ratified in the same city (Philadelphia), in the same building (Independence Hall), and in the same year (1789).

Our polity has the characteristics of a Catholic and Protestant church, very much like our identity and authority. Our catholicity features our three-fold ministry of bishops, priests, and deacons ordained by bishops who stand in line of succession from the apostles, generally called the apostolic succession or historic episcopate. Our protestant characteristics include witness to the fundamental truths of the Gospel, protest against the unique authority of individuals like the Pope, the usage of the vernacular tongue in our worship, and the freedom of conscience of individual Christians. The Episcopal Church is a *via media* between both polities.

Our polity is contained in a small volume (approximately 200 pages) entitled *The Constitution and Canons of the Episcopal Church*. The first edition was published in 1789 and it has been revised every three years when the Episcopal Church meets at its General Convention with all bishops and lay and clerical representatives from every **diocese**. Each of the 109 dioceses of the Episcopal Church also has a constitution and canons to govern its life.

We are neither a church in which a few persons have absolute authority to make unilateral decisions, nor are we a church in which everyone has equal authority to make communal decisions. We understand power as the ability to influence rather than to coerce. We understand authority as the right to be heard rather than the right to be obeyed. While some persons are granted structural authority—that is, the right to be heard because of their office—most often our understanding of authority works best when it is founded upon a person's proven wisdom, moral example, spiritual being, or gifts for ministry.

At our best, those in authority listen carefully to every voice, reflect seriously on every side of an issue, and pray faithfully before they make a decision. When a decision is reached, they communicate as best they can how they arrived at their decision with the hope that while everyone may not agree, everyone will understand why and therefore be willing to accept and support it. In general we believe that important decisions should be made by consensus. A consensus does not mean that everyone wholeheartedly supports a decision, but that everyone can live with it and support it. On those occasions when responsible, representative bodies have believed they must act without consensus, they have deliberately acted to maintain unity by providing some way out for those who cannot in conscience live with or support the decision.

As Episcopalians, we have typically intended to live by the virtues of honesty, loyalty, good manners (being polite, courteous, and gracious), mutual respect, restraint, and patience. Nevertheless, we need also to understand the political structures and organization of our church.

The Local Church

"The Church," as stated in the Book of Common Prayer (p. 854), "is the Body of which Jesus Christ is the Head and of which all baptized persons are members." The ministers of the church are "lay persons, bishops, priests, and deacons" (p. 855). The church is an organization that exists to support and encourage all Christians in their ministries. There is a radical difference between the church and secular organizations, which ordinarily define membership in terms of signed applications, approval for membership, and the payment of dues. Church membership is defined by baptism: no application, no screening process, and no dues. The Episcopal Church takes this very seriously. Membership is a gift of God and the church's role is to welcome and nurture, not to create barriers. Members who are baptized, regularly attend church services, and have been "faithful in working, praying, and giving for the spread of the Kingdom of God" (Canon I.17.2) are considered **communicant** members in good standing.

Members of each **congregation**, or parish, govern locally. A **parish** exists when the worshipping community gathered is self-supporting and contributes proportionally to the ministry of the diocese. Typically, there is an annual meeting in which the members of each congregation come together to elect its **vestry**, or governing body, as well as representatives to diocesan convention. The senior officers of the vestry are called wardens and may be elected by the parish or vestry itself, depending on the congregation's bylaws. Their responsibilities include acting as the ecclesiastical authority in the absence of a **rector**. A treasurer and clerk (secretary) is also elected or appointed. The vestry, presided over by the rector, has jurisdiction for the financial and property aspects of parish life. A congregation that requires financial support from the diocese is known as an aided parish, sometimes called a **mission**. Their clergy leader, called a **vicar**, is appointed by (in consultation with the parish) and fully accountable to the **bishop**.

The annual parish meeting also normally provides opportunity for the members of the congregation to be given a full account of the condition of the parish. The rector or vicar may give an overall picture of the spiritual life of the congregation. The wardens report on the state of the parish from their perspective, the treasurer usually presents a very full financial report, and leaders of church organizations report on their activities. Opportunity is also given for questions and discussion. It is a model of governance that offers inclusion and transparency.

The canons are clear in dividing the responsibility for church life on the local level between the rector or vicar and the vestry. The rector is responsible for the conduct of services (worship and music) and the teaching of the faith. The vestry is assigned the management of finances and property. While the canons say nothing about programmatic elements of a congregation (fellowship, outreach, stewardship, etc.), most vestries appoint committees to supervise various aspects of parish life, working with the rector to carry out these program areas. The rector is also responsible for the presentation of persons for baptism, confirmation, and marriage as well as stewardship education.

One of the most important decisions most congregations need to make is the choice of their clergy leadership, and although the parish does choose its rector, it must have the bishop's advice in the process as well as the bishop's approval of the person selected. When a rector is called to another congregation or retires, the parish forms a search committee to look for a new rector. Meanwhile, the vestry, with the advice of the bishop, will select a priest to serve as an interim during the period between rectors. In consultation with the diocese, the search committee makes a study of the parish and asks its members for their ideas about the needs and opportunities facing the congregation. The search committee uses this information as it reads resumés, visits other Episcopal churches, conducts interviews, and selects a candidate with a recommendation to the vestry. When the vestry has elected a priest and received the bishop's approval, the priest is then formally instituted and cannot be removed without due cause and the bishop's consent.

Other clergy may be called to serve as assistants in a congregation at the request of the rector, in consultation with the vestry. Those who are newly ordained are often called **curates**. Churches often have other paid staff persons to help administer programs and ministries, such as administration, Christian formation, and communication.

The congregations of the Episcopal Church have a considerable degree of independence in managing their affairs. Each may develop a special character in terms of liturgical style, music, and outreach ministries. While all church property is held in trust by the vestry for the diocese, the Episcopal Church assumes that the members of its churches know what is best for the needs of their community.

The Diocese

An Episcopal congregation (parish) is not a congregational (independent) church. It is part of a diocese that may include all or part of a state or country. Dioceses range in size from twenty or thirty parishes to over two hundred. Dioceses are formed with the consent of the General Convention and are the fundamental units of the Episcopal Church.

Each parish pays an assessment or apportionment to their diocese annually for the work of the diocese. This pays the salaries of the bishop and diocesan staff and supports the ministry of the diocese for such tasks as mission churches, youth ministry, education, and training of all its members in its congregations. Every diocese also pays a proportion of their budget to the church-wide body of the Episcopal Church for its work and ministry in the world.

The bishop is the chief pastor of the diocese as well as every parish in the diocese. "The ministry of a bishop is to represent Christ and his Church particularly as apostle, chief priest, and pastor of a diocese" (p. 855). It is impossible for a bishop to be present each Sunday in every congregation, so presbyters (priests) serve at his or her will as personal delegates and representatives to his or her ministry. The Book of Common Prayer states that the responsibilities of a bishop are "to guard the faith, unity, and discipline of the whole Church; to proclaim the Word of God; to act in Christ's name for the reconciliation of the world and the building up of the Church; and to ordain others to continue Christ's ministry" (p. 855).

The work of the diocese is coordinated by an **annual convention** that adopts a budget and program for the coming year. Each congregation sends elected lay delegates to the annual convention, who are joined by all clergy who are resident in the diocese, whether their vocation is in a church or other institution, such as a school, hospital, or agency. At convention, the bishop chairs the gathering. Clergy and lay people are elected to serve on a **diocesan council**. This council (or Executive Board) administers that budget and program. The diocese also elects members to a **Standing Committee**, a group of lay and clerical members who serve as a council of advice and consent to the bishop. This body must approve of all persons to be ordained, consent to the consecration of a bishop in another diocese, approve the sale of all church properties, and in the case when there is no bishop, act as the diocese's ecclesiastical authority. Both the diocesan council and standing committee can be seen as a parallel body to the parish vestry in its responsibilities.

Just as the bishop has a role in a congregation's choice in the selection of priest, the parish has a role in the selection of a bishop. A bishop is elected for life (with a mandatory retirement at age 72) by the diocese meeting as a special body of clergy and representative laity from each congregation. Usually a nominating committee is formed to discern the needs and vision of the diocese as well as receive resumes and interview potential candidates. In some ways this is very similar in how a local congregation seeks a new rector. Convention delegates are given the opportunity to meet selected candidates in advance of the special convention called for an election of a bishop. It is required that a candidate has a majority of the votes of both the clergy and lay delegates.

The Council of Nicaea in 325 C.E. provided that no bishop could be consecrated, except by three other bishops, thus ensuring that the ministry within the church had the approval and support of the larger church. In the Episcopal Church today, the election of a bishop is consecrated by at least three other bishops of the Episcopal Church. For administrative purposes, dioceses are often divided into convocations or deaneries.

Large dioceses may also elect a **suffragan bishop** to assist the bishop, or may call on a retired bishop to serve as an assistant. A bishop approaching retirement age will often ask the diocese to elect a successor, called a **bishop coadjutor**, to serve with him or her in an interim period so that there can be a smooth transition to new leadership.

The bishop's primary pastoral relationship is with the clergy of his or her diocese. **Deacons** serve directly under their bishop, who assigns them to a congregation for liturgical purposes. Deacons are servants to the whole Church, particularly in ministries to the poor, sick, and needy. Liturgically, they assist bishops and priests in the proclamation of the Gospel and the administration of the sacraments.

Lay people can be authorized and licensed by the bishop to serve many roles in a parish. Lay readers can officiate at prayer services, Eucharistic ministers either help to serve communion at services or take communion to those unable to attend Sunday or Holy Day Eucharists. The **laity** can be licensed to preach, and **catechists** are those who prepare persons for baptism, **confirmation**, **reception**, or baptismal renewal. Lectors (read the lessons) and intercessors (lead the Prayers of the People) only need to be authorized by the rector or vicar.

There are four orders of ministry: lay persons, bishops, priests, and deacons. Each has a role to play in the polity of the Episcopal Church.

The Episcopal Church

The Episcopal Church is comprised of 6,700 congregations (1.9 million members) organized in 109 dioceses in nine provinces (composed of a group of geographically adjacent dioceses) throughout the United States, Europe, the Caribbean, Taiwan, Micronesia, and Central and South America.

Since 1789, the General Convention has been the central governing body of the Episcopal Church. Those who created the structure of the Episcopal Church were, in many cases, the same individuals who had framed and adopted the Constitution of the United States only a few years earlier, so it is not surprising that our structure is very similar. Meeting every three years, our legislative body consists of a House of Deputies (lay people and clergy chosen by their dioceses) and the House of Bishops (consisting of all bishops, both active and retired, though not all attend all meetings). Meeting every three years, its primary responsibility includes the maintenance of the Constitution and Canons of the church (governing documents), which are subject to amendment at each convention. Changes to the Constitution and the Book of Common Prayer require the agreement of two consecutive conventions.

In addition to such amendments to church law and liturgy, General Convention will normally consider some hundreds of additional resolutions concerning national and world affairs, interreligious and ecumenical relations, and social issues, among other topics. They also adopt a budget for the triennial (three years). All resolutions are assigned to legislative committees made up of bishops and deputies. They hold open hearings and make recommendations to the House that first votes on each resolution. A majority of both lay and clergy votes is necessary in the House of Deputies. Because the two Houses meet and deliberate separately, all actions must be agreed to by both (in identical language) in order to become law or policy, so if a resolution fails in the House of initial action, it never makes it to the other.

The Episcopal Church is often referred to as the Domestic and Foreign Missionary Society (DFMS). This is the legal body, whose constitution dates back to 1821, that oversees the endowment funds of the Episcopal Church.

The **Presiding Bishop** is the chief pastor and chief executive of the church and is charged by the canons with responsibility to "speak God's words to the Church and to the world, as their representative of this Church and its episcopate in its corporate capacity" (Canon I.2.4[a]). The House of Bishops, with the consent of the House of Deputies, elects him or her every nine years. He or she is also called on to visit every diocese and consult with the bishops and diocesan representatives. Between the sessions of General Convention, the Executive Council, a number of interim committees and commissions, and the staff of the Presiding Bishop work to put the decisions made into effect, and offer proposals for consideration at the next session of the Convention.

Whether it is on the local (parish, mission, congregational), diocesan, or church-wide level of the Episcopal Church, people elected to an office or to a representative body are never sent to a meeting to represent, defend, or vote for a position established by those who elect them or the group they are to represent. They are elected because it is believed that they can think for themselves and deal openly with complex matters. They are also to be spiritually mature enough to listen for the leading of the Spirit so as to be set free to vote their conscience. No proxy votes are acceptable. Those who have been party to the conversation and prayer of the body are called upon to consider a matter and reach the decision.

The Anglican Communion

The Episcopal Church is one of 44 national and regional churches or jurisdictions in 165 countries worldwide that make up the **Anglican Communion**. We're more than 80 million members strong.

We are a loosely based fellowship held together by Jesus Christ and the distinctive beliefs we share, largely as they were spread in the expansion of the British Empire (and later by Americans) and the church that traveled with them, bringing along the Book of Common Prayer. The Communion has no central government, but is loosely linked by four "instruments" of communion: the Archbishop of Canterbury, who has no canonical authority over the Anglican Communion but serves the Church of England as its chief pastor; the Lambeth Conference, a once-a-decade meeting (since 1867) of bishops from around the world to discuss matters of concern; the Primate's Meeting, a smaller and more frequent gathering of the senior bishops from each of the churches; and the Anglican Consultative Council, a representative body of bishops, clergy, and lay leaders from all the churches, primarily focused on the mission work of the whole Anglican Communion.

The Anglican Communion is the third-largest Christian body in the world. All of these churches have prayer books, though they are often written and adapted by each local body, adding a richness and distinction reflective of each culture. It is at the international level that the nature of the church as an organization becomes more difficult to analyze. The various provinces of the Anglican Communion, of which the Episcopal Church is one, have their own patterns of self-government. While the bishops may issue statements of their opinions on matters of national, international, or pastoral concern, each church or province remains free to make its own decisions about its common life.

Conclusion

The Episcopal Church shield is a familiar symbol found on signs, in newspaper ads in cities and towns, and on many a website. It is usually accompanied by the words, "The Episcopal Church Welcomes You," which may summarize who the Episcopal Church is.

The shield and its corresponding Episcopal Church flag were officially adopted by General Convention in 1940 and are rich in symbolism. The shield is usually presented in red, white, and blue. The red cross on a white field is an ancient Christian symbol, white representing the purity of Jesus and red representing his sacrifice on the cross and the blood of the Christian martyrs. The red cross is known as the cross of St. George, patron saint of England, and indicates the Episcopal Church's descent from the Church of England. The blue field in the upper left is the color traditionally associate with the Blessed Virgin Mary and is symbolic of Jesus' human nature, which he received from his mother. The X-shaped cross is the cross of St. Andrew, patron saint of Scotland, and recalls the Episcopal Church's indebtedness to Scottish bishops for the consecration of the first American bishop, Samuel Seabury, in 1784. The St. Andrew's cross is made up of nine smaller cross-crosslets that stand for the representatives of the church in the nine states who met in Philadelphia in 1789 to adopt the Constitution of the Episcopal Church.

Our Episcopal way of life is composed of the integration and application of all these characteristics. Others in the Christian family may share some of them, but together they make our unique Episcopal character. Episcopalians make our contribution to the one, holy, catholic, and apostolic church when we manifest ourselves authentically, understanding our authority, spirituality, temperament, and polity, while acknowledging the important contributions others make to our common life as believers in Jesus Christ and members of his Church.

Besides being an open and affirming church, we are a church steeped in history and tradition that is engaged with the world. Our post-communion prayer expresses our mission as Episcopalians:

> *Almighty and everliving God,*
> *we thank you for feeding us with the spiritual food*
> *of the most precious Body and Blood*
> *of your Son our Savior Jesus Christ;*
> *and for assuring us in these holy mysteries*
> *that we are living members of the Body of your Son,*
> *and heirs of your eternal kingdom.*
> *And now, Father, send us out*
> *to do the work you have given us to do,*
> *to love and serve you*
> *as faithful witnesses of Christ our Lord.*
> *To him, to you, and to the Holy Spirit,*
> *be honor and glory, now and for ever. Amen.*

BCP, P. 366

Glossary

Anglican Communion—The worldwide assembly of churches that are in communion with the Archbishop of Canterbury. Member churches exercise jurisdictional independence but share a common heritage concerning Anglican identity and commitment to Scripture, tradition, and reason as sources of authority.

Anglicanism—The balance and compromise of the *via media* of the Elizabethan settlement between Protestant and Catholic principles. Today it reflects the balance of its devotion to Scripture, tradition, and reason.

Baptism—Full initiation by water and the Holy Spirit into Christ's Body, the Church. (BCP pp. 299-314). A sacrament in the Episcopal Church.

Baptismal Covenant—The rite of Christian initiation (baptism) contains a series of questions, made by all present who affirm belief in the triune God (through the Apostles' Creed) and promise to continue in the Christian fellowship, resist evil and repent, proclaim the gospel, serve Christ in all persons, and strive for justice and peace. (BCP, pp. 304-305).

Bishop, Diocesan—One of three orders of ordained ministry (priests and deacons), charged with the apostolic ministry of representing Christ and his Church as apostle, chief priest, and pastor to a diocese. (BCP p. 855)

Bishop coadjutor—Assistant bishop with the right of succession upon the resignation of the diocesan bishop.

Book of Common Prayer (BCP)—Official book of worship of the Episcopal Church providing liturgical forms, prayers, and instructions so that all members and orders of the Episcopal Church may appropriately share in common worship.

Canon—Derived from the Greek *kanon*, a "measuring rod or rule." (1) The canon of Scripture is the list of inspired books recognized by the church to constitute the Holy Scriptures. (2) Church laws written that provide a code of laws for the governance of the church. (3) Title of the member of a diocesan or cathedral staff.

Catechist—A teacher, lay or ordained, who provides instruction in the Christian faith.

Communicant—(1) One who receives Holy Communion. (2) A member of the church who has received Holy Communion at least three times in the past year and has been faithful in "working, praying, and giving for the spread of the Kingdom of God."

Confirmation—The sacramental rite in which those who have been baptized at an early age "express their mature commitment to Christ and receive strength from the Holy Spirit through prayer and the laying on of hands by a bishop" (BCP, p. 413-419)

Congregation (see also Parish)—A gathering of people for worship. The term may also refer to a parish church, or the people who participate in the life of a worshipping community.

Constitution (and Canons)—The Constitution of the Episcopal Church was first adopted by the General Convention of the Church in 1789. It contains regulations for General Convention, election and jurisdiction of bishops, Standing Committees, the formation of new jurisdictions, the establishment of provinces, ordinations, ecclesiastical courts, and the Book of Common Prayer. (See also Canons)

Curate—The term typically refers to an assisting priest in a parish. Originally used to describe a priest entrusted with the care (or "cure") of souls in a particular area. The term is not used in the Book of Common Prayer or the Constitution and Canons of the Episcopal Church.

Deacon—Members of one of three distinct orders of ordained ministry (with bishops and presbyters/priests). In the Episcopal Church, a deacon exercises a special ministry of servanthood, serving all people and especially those in need.

Diocese—A geographic are a with its churches and clergy overseen by a bishop. The word was originally used in the Roman Empire for an administrative subdivision. The Constitution and Canons of the Episcopal Church provide guidelines for the division of a diocese. Some would say that the diocese is the primary unit in the Episcopal Church.

Diocesan Council (sometimes called Diocesan Convention)—The yearly gathering of clergy and lay representatives of congregations, with the bishop, to undertake the business of the diocese, including the election of members to church bodies and the ratification of an annual diocesan budget.

Eucharist—The sacrament of Christ's Body and Blood and the principal act of Christian worship. The term is from the Greek, "thanksgiving." Also known as Holy Communion, the Lord's Supper, or the Mass.

General Convention—The church-wide legislative body of the Episcopal Church. It consists of a House of Bishops and House of Deputies that meet every three years.

Historic episcopacy—The unbroken line of bishops ordained by other bishops in a line that goes back to the apostles.

Incarnation—The term that reflects the Christological doctrine that Jesus was fully human and fully divine, the Son of God "in the flesh" based on John 1:14, "And the Word became flesh and lived among us."

Laity (also known as lay persons)—The people of God. The term is from the Greek *laos*, "the people." Generally referred to as people of the church who have not been ordained. They are listed first in the orders of ministry: lay, bishop, priest, and deacon. (See BCP p. 855).

Liturgy—The church's public prayer and worship of God, derived from the Greek words for "people" and "work."

Mission—(1) From the Latin, "to send," Christian mission is the sending forth to proclaim the Gospel of Jesus Christ; (2) A congregation that is financially dependent on a diocese.

Parish (see also Congregation)—A self-supporting congregation under a rector, as opposed to a mission or other congregation under a vicar. A term from English canon law, a parish is an area under the spiritual care of a priest. The term is used without any specific definition other than a "Congregation of this Church" in the canons of the Episcopal Church and is not used as frequently as in past decades.

Presiding Bishop—Chief pastor and primate for the Episcopal Church who has a term of office of nine years.

Reason—One of the three sources of authority in the Episcopal Church, along with scripture and tradition. Reason interprets Scripture and tradition and allows itself to be corrected and enlarged by them. It draws upon the entirety of human understanding and experience.

Reception—Baptized persons who have been members of another Christian fellowship and who wish to be affiliated with the Episcopal Church may make a public affirmation of their faith and commitment to the responsibilities of their baptism in the presence of a bishop. (BCP, p. 418)

Reconciliation of a Penitent—A sacramental rite in which those who repent may confess their sins to God in the presence of a priest and receive the assurance of pardon and the grace of absolution. (BCP, p. 446-452)

Rector—The priest in charge of a self-supporting parish or congregation.

Sacraments—Outward and visible signs of inward and spiritual grace, given by Christ as sure and certain means for receiving God's grace. In the Episcopal Church, Baptism and Eucharist are the two great sacraments.

Scripture—From the Latin for "writings," this word refers to a collection of the most important documents in a given religious community. For the Episcopal Church, this includes the Old Testament, New Testament, and the Apocrypha (BCP p. 853)

Standing Committee—The ecclesiastical authority of a diocese in the absence of a bishop, who are elected by the diocesan convention and consist of clergy and lay persons. They are also serve as a bishop's council of advice on a variety of matters.

Suffragan Bishop—An assisting bishop who does not automatically succeed a diocesan bishop.

Tradition—In Christian theology, originally referred to simply as that which has been handed down to the church through the centuries from the prophets, apostles and their successors, and the authorized teaching of church councils. It joins Scripture and reason as the balance of a source of authority in the Episcopal Church.

Transcendent—Of God, existing apart and not subject to the limitations of the material universe.

Vestry—The legal representative of a parish with regard to all matters pertaining to its corporate property, elected at the annual parish meeting by members of the congregation.

Via Media—Latin phrase translated as "middle way" or the "way between two extremes." It is recognized as a more adequate expression of truth between the weaknesses of extreme positions.

Vicar—The priest in charge of a supported mission congregation. Historically, as early as twelfth-century England, clergy known as vicars were appointed to act as substitutes or vicarious representatives of the bishop to serve congregations.